SEACOAST MAINE

SEACOAST MAINE

PHOTOGRAPHS BY GEORGE TICE

INTRODUCTION BY JOHN K. HANSON

An Imago Mundi Book

DAVID R. GODINE · PUBLISHER

BOSTON

An Imago Mundi Book
published in 2009 by
DAVID R. GODINE · *Publisher*
Post Office Box 450
Jaffrey, New Hampshire 03452
www.godine.com

LIBRARY OF CONGRESS CATALOGING-IN-PUBLICATION DATA

Tice, George A.
Seacoast Maine / photographs by George Tice ; introduction by John K. Hanson. — 1st ed.
p. cm. — (An imago mundi book)
ISBN 978-156792-376-6 (HC)
ISBN 978-156792-378- (SC)
1. Atlantic Coast (Me.)—Pictorial works. 2. Landscape—Maine—Atlantic Coast—Pictorial works.
3. Maine--Pictorial works. I. Title.
F27.A75T43 2009
974.10094′60222—dc22
2008042263

PAGE 2: *Rowboat, Thomaston, 1970*
OPPOSITE: *Gulls off Port Clyde, 1971*

FIRST EDITION, 2009
Printed in the United States of America

To my son Christopher

Russ Island, 1971

INTRODUCTION

A few years ago, an art museum in Katonah, New York, held a summer show featuring the work of Maine artists. From the perspective of a summer-in-the-city resident of Manhattan, the images of Maine by the likes of Louise Nevelson, Rockwell Kent, Frederick Edwin Church, Fairfield Porter, the Wyeths, and others make the state seem a yearned-for place often remote in time, beauty, and subject matter. In other words, an unattainable ideal, a myth – and that is how the exhibition was described in the catalogue *The Myth of Maine as America's Eden*.

The photographs by George Tice in his *Seacoast Maine* also portray a Maine of myth. His portrayal is not of yearning but of belonging – of truths greater than reality. Yes, he has images highlighting the permanence of Maine's rocky coast, the constant movement of the sea, and the efforts of the people who live and work there. But it is not the soft summer light that bathes his extraordinary black-and-white images of life on the coast; it is the colder light of the working day. His photographs show the nobility of tools, the demands of hard work, the challenges of place.

George Tice is from New Jersey. He lives in the Atlantic Highlands area near Sandy Hook Bay – the southern approaches to New York Harbor – though he is very much tied to Paterson, a working-class town in northern New Jersey. Paterson is the subject of two of his earlier books, which reveal a city of immigrants, now-closed mills, and a majestic, seventy-seven-foot waterfall that once powered the mills that were the source of the city's prosperity. His photographs project a stillness that seems to bore into Paterson's core. They inform the details of life there, not with the morbid fascination often seen in the work of other contemporary photographers, but with a more sympathetic "you are there" point of view. The grit is neither glamorized nor fetishized. The photographs of life in Paterson are caught in great detail and in great light.

It is this eye and sense of place that Tice brought with him when he first started to photograph Maine in the summer of 1970, not long before I, with my own New Jersey roots, moved to the state. The photographs in this book span my life in Maine.

I didn't realize it at the time, but it was his early photographs of Maine that helped establish

my personal mythology of the state, my understanding of life on the coast, my sense of place. These images of his, especially the beautiful geometric shot of the porch and the sea on page 11, were on display in galleries along the coast during my first summer there. They helped form my lasting image of Maine's immediate past.

The early seventies were an amazingly creative time along the coast. *Maine Times*, founded by Peter Cox and John Cole in Brunswick in 1969, chronicled the changes; WBLM, "The Blimp," broadcasted the rock-'n'-roll soundtrack; Robert J. Lurtsema intoned the meaning of the classics every morning on public radio, and residents all along the coast from Kittery to Calais began using the traditions of Maine life as a starting point for the new "post-industrial society" that John Cole described and predicted.

The Maine coast was alive with activity. The boatbuilding industry, which had almost died, came to life through the combination of the newly imposed two-hundred-mile territorial limit to keep out foreign fishing vessels and encourage the domestic fleet, and a growing interest in workboat-derived pleasure boats. Old shops were revived and, more importantly, new ones were established. The organic farming and gardening movement started to take root. New publishing ventures, such as *Maine Antique Digest*, *Farmstead*, and *WoodenBoat* were passing on the knowledge of traditional ways and technologies, reenergizing these venerable crafts for new and growing audiences. This revival of old-time traditions helped build the more prosperous Maine of today.

George Tice's photographs speak to me of that era. A goodly number of the photographs in *Seacoast Maine* depict the end of winter or the hint of spring. The trees are bare, there's dirty snow by the edge of the road; this could be the state at what might seem its ugliest. To me, though, this time of year and Tice's photographs speak of a coming renewal. There's a feeling of expectancy: Behind that shop door, a new boat awaits launching as soon as the snow melts; down in Stonington, the lobster boats, ashore for the winter, are poised on the brink of a new season. The long period of dormancy is almost over.

George Tice's images of the sea and the rocky shore are timeless. Even photographs taken in the 1970s of people living and working are as right today as they were thirty-five years ago. The men at work on the fish pier (page 29), the man shoveling bait (page 81), Bertram Peabody and

his son digging clams (page 34) – these photographs and others like them could have been taken today. But then again, they couldn't. The photographs Tice took of the working fishing harbors in the early 1970s were of a time just before the boom began. Yes, the moored boats were usually lobster boats, but there is nevertheless a big difference between those then and those now. The lobster boats of the 1970s were smaller and made of wood, the last generation so built. They were narrower, had engines of much less horsepower, and were designed to fish fewer traps.

Look at Tice's photograph of lobster boats rolling in surge off Monhegan Island (page 21). A wonderful combination of motion and stillness, the image is also a valuable documentation of a working fleet before the wider, bigger, turbo-charged, diesel-powered fiberglass boats became the norm. Today's harbors have more boats, both commercial and recreational, than those depicted in Tice's earliest Maine work. His art documents an earlier, a simpler, and perhaps a happier era before GPS replaced the compass and dead reckoning.

There have been many changes along the coast of Maine in the last thirty-five years. Because of technology – first there was radio, then television, then video, then cable TV, and now the Internet – Maine is no longer as isolated as in decades past. Dance tunes, YouTube, Facebook, and bloggers speed through Maine's ether in a nanosecond, just as everywhere else in the world. This state, however, has not given up its distinction of being a separate, distinctive place. Looking at these images by George Tice, I can still see what makes coastal Maine timeless, as appealing and seductive today as it was four decades ago.

This spring, on a gray day with snow still in the woods, my family and I went to the launching of a wooden lobster boat. The boat was sitting in the cradle of a marine railway; the entire assembled community was waiting for high tide; the children were putting pennies on the rails. The owner was happy, the builders were happy, and I was happy that certain things in Maine never change.

<div align="right">

JOHN K. HANSON
Publisher, Maine Boats, Homes & Harbors

</div>

Porch, Monhegan Island, 1971

Cormorants off Port Clyde, 1971

Window, Port Clyde, 1971

Russ Island, 1971

Sea Fringe, Mount Desert Island, 1971

Russ Island, 1971

17

Island off Port Clyde, 1970

Boat Landing to Monhegan Island, Port Clyde, 1970

Scarecrow, Starboard, 1971

Lobster Boats off Monhegan Island, 1971

Clothesline, Monhegan Island, 1971

23

Wave, Mount Desert Island, 1971

Granite, Mount Desert Island, 1971

Tourist Cabins, Searsport, 1971

27

Nubble Light, Cape Neddick, 1971

Wharf, Jonesport, 1971

29

Evening Fog, Jonesport, 1971

Monhegan Boat Landing, 1971

Mr. and Mrs. Alvah Thompson, Port Clyde, 1971

Bertram Peabody and Son Clamdigging, Beals Island, 1971

Vernon Woodward and James Polk, Jonesport, 1971

Olsen House, Cushing, 1970

Painted Lobster Buoys, Stonington, 1971

37

House in Fog, Jonesport, 1971

Lobster Boat, Stonington, 1971

Houses, Southport, 1971

41

Lobster Traps, Port Clyde, 1970

Ralph Brown, Jonesport, 1971

The Catherine-Beverly, Port Clyde, 1971

Webb's Auto Supply, Stonington, 1971

Walt Anderson, Port Clyde, 1971

Cathedral Woods, Monhegan Island, 1971

49

Cliffs, Quoddy Head, 1971

Lionel Barbour, Stonington, 1971

51

Road to Deer Isle, 1971

House by the Sea, Stonington, 1971

Bathroom, Alma Heal's Hotel, Port Clyde, 1971

Window, Olsen House, Cushing, 1970

Pemaquid Light, Pemaquid Point, 1970

Port Clyde at Sunset, 1971

Shaker Interior, Sabbathday Lake, 1971

63

Encircled Tree, Sargenty, 1971

Shakers at Dinner, Sabbathday Lake, 1971

Morning Fog, Jonesport, 1971

Interior, Sabbathday Lake, 1971

White Church, Stonington, 1971

Stonington Harbor, 1971

Interior, Monhegan Island, 1971

70

Fishing Boat in Fog, Port Clyde, 1970

71

Rowboat, Port Clyde, 1970

Jamie Wyeth, Monhegan Island, 1971

Boatyard Detail, Thomaston, 1971

75

Schooner off Mount Desert Island, 1970

Cliffs, Quoddy Head, 1971

Grain Elevator, Portland, 1971

Unloading Bait, Friendship, 1971

Young's Furniture Store, Portland, 1971

Keenan's Barber Shop, Portland, 1971

Wallace Market, Friendship, 1971

Lobster Pots and Buoys, Monhegan Island, 1971

Dwight Stanley, Monhegan Island, 1971

Interior, Olsen House, Cushing, 1971

View of Stonington, 1971

Road, Edgecomb, 1971

Tourist Cabin, Port Clyde, 1970

Woods, Stonington, 1971

Two Lights, Cape Elizabeth, 1971

International Bridge to Campobello Island, Lubec, 1971

Otter Cliffs, Mount Desert Island, 1971

97

Rock Wall, Mount Desert Island, 1970

Mount Desert Island, 1970

Shore in Fog, Mount Desert Island, 1970

102

Woods, Port Clyde, 1970

Mount Desert Island, 1970

Submerged Rock, Port Clyde, 1978

Lone Tree, Orland, 1981

Farmhouse in Fog, St. George, 1982

Fish House, Stonington, 1984

Winter Street, Rockport, 1984

Tourists, Stonington, 1984

Low Tide, Mount Desert Island, 1989

Portland Head Light, Cape Elizabeth, 1995

Sunset, Rockport, 1987

Granite Detail, Mosquito Head, 1995

Shrouded Boat, Thomaston, 1994

Lake Near Camden, 2000

Lobsterman's Cottage, Beals Island, 1999

Bus Stop, Belfast, 1990

Wind-blown Grasses, Searsport, 2000

Lobster Shacks, Beals Island, 2000

Trees in Fog, Pembroke, 2000

Sunrise, Beals Island, 2000

Island Ferry, Rockland, 2000

Farmhouse, Lubec, 2000

Camden Harbor, 2001

Wharf, Beals Island, 2000

Camden Harbor, 2005

Cottage, East Machias, 2007

Bird on Wire, Mount Desert Island, 2007

Portland Seaport, 2007

Machias River, Machias, 2007

Seacoast, Sullivan, 2007

Ring Bolt, Stonington, 1984

Seacoast Maine

has been set in Monotype Dante, a face designed by the renowned scholar, typographer, and printer, Giovanni Mardersteig, for use at his Officina Bodoni in Verona, Italy. The types were cut in the 1950s by Charles Malin, the French punchcutter whose collaboration with Mardersteig produced a series of distinctive faces over a span of twenty-five years. The Dante type takes as its models the Italian types of the fifteenth century, but the deftness of Mardersteig's drawing and the brilliance of Malin's cutting save the type from the excessive refinement that limits the usefulness of many faces cut for private presses.

Thanks to Claudia Ansorge, Sally Arteseros, Edward L. Deci, Jennifer Delaney, Deborah Delzotti, Martin Dibner, Harvey Dwight, David R. Godine, John K. Hanson, Tom Ives and Lois M. Tristaino of New Hampshire Bindery, August Kleinzahler, Joan LaBanca, Carl W. Scarbrough, Lisa Tice, Earl Tidwell, Marie Tremmel, Bob Tursack of Brilliant Graphics, and Jamie Wyeth.

DESIGN BY GEORGE TICE AND CARL W. SCARBROUGH